# GATEWAYS

## Anthony Mauk

Chapin Keith Publishing
Daleville, VA. 24083
www.chapinkeith.com

Publisher's Cataloging-in-Publication Data

Names: Mauk, Anthony - author.
Title: Gateways / Anthony Mauk

Identifiers: LCCN: 2023922136 | ISBN: 979-8-9893575-2-9 (Hardcover) |
979-8-9893575-1-2 (Paperback) | 979-8-9893575-3-6 (eBook)
BISAC POETRY / General | POETRY/ American/General |


Cover and book design by Asya Blue Design

All photos including the cover are by Anthony Mauk except as noted

First Edition

# FOREWORD

I first met Anthony "Tony" Mauk in 2008 or 2009 while managing a business unit for Cobham Defense Electronics in Blacksburg, Virginia. Tony was a sales and marketing executive based in Southern California, representing Cobham and other companies. During that meeting, I was struck not only by his competence and expertise, but also his genuineness and the lively spirit behind his professionalism. I found it ironic when I learned that he was a native of nearby Roanoke, Virginia, living in Southern California where I was born and raised.

After I left Cobham in 2011 for another position and eventually to pursue my interest in writing, Tony and I reconnected a few years later on Facebook. To my delight and surprise, I discovered that this successful businessman also had a passion for poetry and photography. As I read some of his heartfelt verses and took in the beauty of his nature photography, I realized there were deeper layers to this man than I originally understood during our time conducting business.

The idea for this collection emerged earlier in 2023 when Tony approached me about publishing some of his excellent photographic and poetic work. Having long felt that his poems deserve to be shared with a wider audience, I was excited at the opportunity.

For those less familiar with Tony's professional background, he has built an impressive career over several decades in the aerospace and defense sphere. Yet his resume and list of work accomplishments only reveal a portion of this Renaissance man's talents. As illustrated by the pieces compiled in this book, Tony also has a deep sensitivity to the written word and the visual world. The images he captures with his camera express vibrancy and care for the natural landscapes and creatures around us every day that we often overlook or take for granted. His poems give language to universal human experiences like love, grief, joy, spirituality, and aging with insight and eloquence.

I am proud to introduce the work of my friend and colleague Tony Mauk in this collection showcasing his twin gifts with verse and film. I hope the unique combination of words and image these pages present allows you to catch a glimpse into the same warm personality and creative spark I have come to admire over our years of connection. Please enjoy this showcase offering only a sample of Tony's decades of photography alongside more recent poetic efforts, as his artistic talents continue to develop and unfold.

Ken Conklin
President of Chapin Keith Publishing and author of
*NORVEL: An American Hero* and his own poetry collection, *The Zen of Ken*

# TABLE OF CONTENTS

# MORNING MOON

Morning moon, in the sky,
Clouds pass by, so high
Shining bright, in the night
The moonlight so white
A peaceful sight, so sublime
The beauty of the morning moon, in time

*2023*

# POINT VICENTE LIGHTHOUSE

Point Vicente Lighthouse
Fog horns at night, a mournful sound
The sea is still, the air is dense
The misty fog is all around
The sky is dark and the air is still
The lonesome fog horns sound
Their mournful sound so low
The haunting call is heard so clear
On this dark and silent night
The fog horns call out in the night
Their lonely sound so deep
The haunting call is heard so clear
On this dark and silent night
The fog horns call out in the night
Their lonely sound so deep
The sound of fog horns at night
Will bring peace and solace to me.

*2010*

# VILLA NARCISSA

The Villa Narcissa stands proud,
Built by Frank and Narcissa Vanderlip
It's beauty can be seen from miles around,
With panoramic views of ocean and sound.
The details were crafted with care,
No expense was spared,
The love and passion that was put in,
Will last for generations to come.
The Villa Narcissa stands tall,
A testament to the love of two,
For it is their legacy that lives on,
In the majestic Villa Narcissa.

*2023 – Dedicated to the Vanderlip Family*

# SUNSETS OVER PALOS VERDES

The sunsets over Palos Verdes,
My heart is filled with joy and bliss.
The waves crash against the shore,
My love for this place grows more and more.
The rolling hills, the salty air,
The views of the ocean from anywhere.
The endless beauty, the peacefulness,
My love for Palos Verdes will never cease.

*2023*

# THE SEAGULL

The seagull soars high in the sky,
The sun blazing bright in the sky,
The seagull glides in the air,
The sun warming the air.
The seagull and sun in harmony,
The seagull and sun in unity,
The seagull and sun in perfect harmony,
A beautiful sight for all to see.

---

*2014*

# REFLECTING MOON

The moon is so bright,
It's reflecting off the sea,
A sight so beautiful,
In Palos Verdes for me.
The night sky is alive,
The stars twinkle and shine,
What a special place,
Where I can take my time.
The waves crash and roar,
The wind a gentle breeze,
The beauty of the ocean,
A sight I can't believe.
The moon is so full,
It glows with a golden hue,
A breathtaking view,
In Palos Verdes for me
and you.

*2017*

# INDONESIA

In the land of beauty, where palm trees sway,
In Indonesia's embrace, my family does lay.
With hearts so humble, they light up the scene,
In their humble abodes, a love serene.
Oh, my beautiful family, a treasure untold,
In your presence, warmth and love unfold.
From the shores of Bali to Java's grace,
Your spirits shine, leaving trails of embrace.
Amidst the beaches, where the waves gently crash,
In your laughter and smiles, joy does thrash.
With every sunset painting the sky,
Your love and unity reach new highs.
In the depths of traditions, stories are shared,
Generations intertwined, a legacy so revered.
From Sumatra's jungles to Sulawesi's might,
Your roots run deep, embracing the light.
Oh, Indonesia's children, proud and strong,
In your diverse tapestry, we all belong.
Through trials and triumphs, you stand tall,
Uniting as one, answering the call.
In your humble abodes, love finds its way,
A refuge of peace, where hearts can stray.
From the palm trees' shade to the ocean's breeze,
Your bond as a family will never cease.
So here's to my beautiful Indonesian kin,
A tapestry of love, where memories begin.
In your land of beaches and palm trees so grand,
May love and harmony forever expand.

---

*Oct 2023*

# OCTOBER FIELDS

In Virginia's land, majestic and grand,
The farms unfold, a picturesque band.
The backbone of America, these farmers true,
Their stock market thrives, with cows, horses, and pigs too.
They toil with pride, generations tough,
Devoted and resilient, their spirits enough.
Survivors they are, through trials they've tread,
These farmers of Virginia, where strength is widespread.
Mountains so colorful, a sight to behold,
Over meandering fields, stories untold.
Wheat, corn, and alfalfa, waving in the breeze,
Nature's bounty, a tapestry that never cease.
Balancing the year, a delicate dance,
Stored food sustains, a vital chance.
For spring and summer, fresh foods they sow,
Nourishing the land, as the seasons flow.
The farms of Virginia, a testament profound,
Where beauty and hard work harmoniously abound.
With every sunrise, a promise anew,
The farmers of this land, their legacy true.

---

*Oct 2023*

Courtesy of Robin R. Scott.

# OCTOBER SKIES

In the vast canvas of endless skies,
Where nature's artistry truly lies,
A symphony of colors starts to unfold,
Painting stories, both new and old.
Patel blues, like whispers of dreams,
Embrace the heavens in gentle streams,
While squirls of orange, a fiery dance,
Illuminate the sky in a vibrant trance.
In those precious moments, morning or late,
When sunrays pierce through heaven's gate,
A kaleidoscope of hues, a glorious array,
Reveals the mood of nature's display.
For on stormy days, when dark clouds brew,
The sky weeps tears of a somber hue,
Raindrops fall, like nature's gentle plea,
Washing the world, setting spirits free.
And when the wind howls with wild delight,
Clouds race across the canvas, taking flight,
Their shapes and forms, ever-changing, grand,
Creating masterpieces across the land.
The best paintings, indeed, are filled with clouds,
Whispering secrets, their mysteries allowed,
They add depth and character to the scene,
Transforming the ordinary into the serene.
So let us marvel at the sky's painted grace,
The ever-shifting palette nature embraces,
For in those fleeting moments of divine art,
We find solace and wonder in our heart.

---

*2023*

# MOUNTAINS OF VIRGINIA

In the heart of Virginia's embrace,
Where mountains rise with tranquil grace,
I weave a poem of scenic delight,
Of tree frogs singing through the night.
Oh, Virginia's mountains, majestic and high,
A testament to nature's grand design,
With peaks that touch the azure sky,
And valleys where dreams intertwine.
Amidst these ancient, misty peaks,
Where nature's harmony softly speaks,
Reside the tree frogs in their abode,
Their symphony, a melodious ode.
As twilight falls and stars emerge,
Their chorus swells, a vibrant surge,
Their tender songs, a soothing balm,
Echoing through the tranquil calm.
In this land of verdant green,
A tapestry of life can be seen,
Hardworking souls with calloused hands,
Rooted deep in these fertile lands.
From the bustling cities to rural abodes,
Where life's rhythm beats, it surely shows,
The tireless toil on fertile soil,
A testament to their unwavering coil.
From the coal mines of Appalachia's might,
To the farms that yield abundance bright,
Virginia's sons and daughters stand tall,
Their spirit resilient, never to fall.
So, let us honor this cherished land,
Its mountains, where nature's wonders expand,

And praise the tree frogs' harmonious plea,
And the hardworking people, strong and free.
In the mountains of Virginia, a haven so dear,
Where tree frogs sing, and hard work is near,
Let us celebrate the beauty that thrives,
In this land where nature and labor connive.

_____

*1988*

Courtesy of Robin R Scott.

# CHILDREN OF AFRICA

Where tender hearts find their embrace,
A poem now blooms, sincere and wild,
To celebrate each cherished child.
With eyes like stars, so full of wonder,
They light our lives with love's sweet thunder.
Their laughter dances, like melodies divine,
In every corner of this heart of mine.
Oh, the beauty that their spirits hold,
More precious than the purest gold.
Their innocence, a gentle breeze,
Whispering secrets among the trees.
In their smiles, the sun does rise,
Dispelling darkness with radiant skies.
Their tiny hands, so soft and small,
Hold the power to heal and enthral.
With every step, they paint the world anew,
Their dreams and hopes in colors true.
In their presence, we find solace rare,
And burdens lift as they joyfully share.
Through every stumble, every fall,
We stand beside them, strong and tall.
For love knows not the bounds of time,
It weaves a bond that's so sublime.
We nurture their dreams, we guide their way,
With love as our compass, come what may.
For in their hearts, our legacy lies,
A testament to love that never dies.
So let us cherish these precious souls,
Embrace them tightly, make them whole.
For in the depths of their innocent eyes,
We glimpse a love that never denies.

This poem is a testament to the love we hold,
For our children, more valuable than gold.
May their spirits soar, their dreams take flight,
Forever cherished, in our hearts' warm light.

# CHILDREN AROUND THE WORLD

For the Love of our children
In the realm of love's purest grace,
Where tender hearts find their embrace,
A poem now blooms, sincere and wild,
To celebrate each cherished child.
With eyes like stars, so full of wonder,
They light our lives with love's sweet thunder.
Their laughter dances, like melodies divine,
So let us cherish these precious souls,
Embrace them tightly, make them whole.
For in the depths of their innocent eyes,
We glimpse a love that never denies.
This poem is a testament to the love we hold,
For our children, more valuable than gold.
May their spirits soar, their dreams take flight,
Forever cherished, in our hearts' warm light.

Courtesy of Sheri Harrison

# THE DRAGON FLOWER

In a garden of wonders, where colors dance,
A dragon fruit flower, in vibrant romance,
A beacon of beauty, with petals so bright,
Like golden sunbeams, it dazzles the sight.
A celestial creation, ablaze with pure gold,
Its radiance captivating, a story untold,
Each petal unfurls, with grace and allure,
A symphony of yellow, so vivid and pure.
The sun's precious gift, in a world so rare,
A flower of marvel, beyond compare,
It blooms with splendor, a celestial embrace,
A testament of nature's artistic grace.
The fragrance it carries, a sweet-scented hymn,
Whispering secrets, on a gentle breeze's whim,
The bees come aflutter, drawn to its charms,
Serenading its beauty, with delicate psalms.
Oh, dragon fruit flower, a treasure divine,
Your luminescent petals, forever will shine,
Like the sun in the heavens, you proudly proclaim,
A symbol of joy, in nature's grand game.
So, let us rejoice, in this golden delight,
Embrace its brilliance, with hearts taking flight,
For in this humble marvel, we're reminded anew,
Of the wonders that flourish, in nature's debut.

*2023*

# THE OCEAN AND THE SEAGULL

In the realms where sky and ocean unite,
A tale unfolds, bathed in golden light.
Of a seagull, graceful with wings unfurled,
And the mighty sun, ruler of the world.
High above the azure waves it soared,
With a spirit free, untamed and adored.
Its feathers kissed by the salt-laden breeze,
As it danced with the waves, a sight to please.
The seagull's eyes beheld the radiant sun,
A celestial orb, a blazing one.
Its fiery rays painted the heavens above,
Igniting the world with life and love.
Enchanted by the sun's ethereal glow,
The seagull yearned, its heart all aglow.
To reach the sun, to touch its vibrant face,
And bask in its warmth, in that lofty space.
With wings of determination, it took flight,
Ascending towards the sun, a daring sight.
But the closer it soared, the sun remained afar,
A distant beacon, an untouchable star.
Undeterred, the seagull pressed on with might,
Embracing the challenge, pursuing the light.
For even if the sun seemed out of reach,
Its shimmering essence taught lessons to teach.
The sun, ever watchful, saw the seagull's plight,
A creature of courage, a symbol of flight.
It smiled upon the seagull, gentle and kind,
And whispered, "Dear bird, your spirit's aligned."
"For I am the sun, the source of your dreams,
I illuminate life's ever-flowing streams.
Though you can't touch me in your earthly flight,

My warmth and brilliance guide you with light."
The seagull, humbled, embraced the sun's decree,
Accepting its place, finding solace in the sea.
For the sun's radiance still adorned its wings,
And within its heart, the joy of the sun sings.
Through the vast expanse, they forever remain,
The seagull and the sun, an eternal refrain.
A tale of resilience, of dreams and devotion,
Unfolding in harmony, an eternal ocean.

*2023*

# THE WINDMILL AND THE MOON

In days gone by, a windmill stood,
Its weathered sails in the neighborhood.
With creaking gears and spinning grace,
It danced with the wind, in an endless chase.
Tall and proud, a relic of the past,
Whispering stories that forever last.
Its weathered wood told tales untold,
Of farmers, dreams, and fortunes old.
Through golden fields, the breeze would blow,
Caressing the mill with a gentle flow.
It harnessed the wind, a tireless friend,
Turning the gears, a cycle without end.
And as the sun dipped below the hill,
The moon emerged, serene and still.
Ancient and wise, a celestial guide,
A beacon of light, shining far and wide.
The moon, an observer, never grows old,
Its face unchanged, a story untold.
It witnessed empires rise and fall,
Yet remained constant, above us all.
Together they danced, the wind and the moon,
A timeless waltz, in harmony attune.
The windmill spun, the moonbeams glowed,
A symphony of wonders, nature bestowed.
Oh, windmill of days gone by,
With your tales that touch the sky,
And moon, ever constant and bright,
Eternal guardian of the night.

May your spirits forever endure,
In the hearts of dreamers, pure.
For in your presence, we find solace deep,
And memories that we'll forever keep.

---

*2023*

# THE MOON AND THE BELL

In the realm where dreams are woven,
Where enchantment's veils unfurl,
Dwells a tale of moon and bell,
In their dance, a cosmic swirl.
High above the earthly realm,
The moon, serene and bright,
Casts its silver-gilded rays,
Illuminating the depths of night.
Every cycle, twenty-seven days,
With grace, it waxes and wanes,
Guiding sailors through the dark,
As the ocean's lullaby maintains.
But beneath the moon's celestial glow,
A bell resonates its timeless chime,
A faithful guardian of earthly realms,
A marker of moments, a rhythmic rhyme.
With each resounding toll, it echoes,
Through bustling streets and quiet dell,
Announcing dawn's awakening,
And bidding dusk its fond farewell.
Amidst the bustling city's hum,
The bell's melodic voice rings clear,
Guiding us through the passing hours,
From dawn's embrace to twilight's sheer.
It echoes through the hallowed halls,
Where prayers and solace intertwine,
A call to gather, to seek solace,
In the sacred spaces, divine.
But the moon and the bell, intertwined,
Their roles, though different, coincide,
For while one guides the sailor's way,
The other helps us stay aligned.

The moon, the mistress of the tide,
Pulls the waters with a gentle hand,
Assisting fishermen in their quests,
Navigating the dark, uncharted land.
And as the bell tolls, its voice resounds,
Marking the hours, the days that flow,
Reminding us of life's swift passage,
And the moments we hold close, aglow.
So, let us cherish the moon and bell,
These celestial guides, steadfast and true,
For in their luminous embrace,
They weave a tapestry of time anew.
As the moon cycles and tides entwine,
And the bell's toll chimes with love's decree,
We find rhythm in the cosmic dance,
And embrace the grace of eternity.

*2023*

# MARRIAGE

When marriage takes flight, two paths unfold,
Each with its own story, yet intertwined and bold.
One path may soar high, reaching for the sky,
While the other may wander, seeking reasons why.
In the first flight, communication is key,
Open hearts and minds, where both souls are free.
They navigate together, hand in hand,
Guided by love and a shared understanding.
But on the second flight, a change takes place,
Where communication falters, leaving an empty space.
The winds of doubt and misunderstanding blow,
And the once clear skies become clouded, you know.
Yet, even in this turbulence, hope can be found,
For love has the power to turn things around.
With patience and forgiveness, they can mend,
And find their way back to love's sweet blend.
So, let us remember, when marriage takes flight,
To nurture the bond, keeping love in sight.
For in communication and change, lies the key,
To a journey of love that's meant to be.

---

*Sept 2023*

Courtesy of Tom Brogan

# LOVE

In the realm of love, where dreams take flight,
You are the beacon, my guiding light.
With every beat, my heart ignites,
In your embrace, love's pure delight.
Your presence, like a symphony of grace,
Fills my world with beauty, every space.
No words can capture, no verse can tell,
The depth of love, in which we dwell.
In the vast expanse of love's embrace,
You are my shelter, my saving grace.
No distance can diminish, no time erode,
The love we share, forever bestowed.
In the universe of love, you're my star,
Guiding me, no matter how far.
With you, my love, my thoughts align,
For in my heart, eternally, you shine.

*2023*

# LOVE HEALS

In a time when we were lost and broken,
Our hearts shattered, words unspoken.
But now we stand, stronger than before,
Learning from the past, we'll seek no more.
Though pain seeped in, and boughs did break,
We'll mend our wounds, for our own sake.
No need for sorry, for mistakes made,
For in forgiveness, new paths are laid.
We once stood still, hearts filled with chill,
But now we rise, against our own will.
A stranger came, but love we'll find,
Within ourselves, our souls aligned.
No fool tears love apart, we'll mend,
With open hearts, our wounds will tend.
No heavy heart, no burden to bear,
We'll find solace, love beyond compare.
We'll cherish memories, both joy and pain,
For they have shaped us, made us regain.
With love as our guide, we'll find our way,
Towards a brighter, more hopeful day.
No fool tears love apart, we'll rise,
With strength and grace, we'll reach the skies.
For deep within our souls, we know,
Love will heal us, and help us grow.

_____

*Sept 2023*

# CARS

The era of cars from the 1940s,
And the 1950s sock hops with twists,
We danced to the tunes of Buddy Holly,
And rocked the night away, oh so jolly.
Cruising down the streets on warm summer nights,
Underneath the starry skies, such delights,
The Peppermint Club, where we'd all gather,
Listening to Bill Deal and the Rhondels, rather.
The melodies filled the air, so sweet,
As we moved our feet to the rhythmic beat,
Chubby Checkers' twist had us all grooving,
Memories of those times are truly soothing.
Those were the days of innocence and fun,
Where friendships were formed, never to be undone,
So let's raise a toast to those golden years,
And cherish the memories, forever dear.

––––––––––

*2023*

# EVENING SKIES

In the canvas of the evening sky,
Hues of blue, orange, and grey collide,
A pastel masterpiece, oh so high,
Painted by nature's gentle stride.
The blue, serene and calm above,
Like a tranquil sea, it softly shines,
Embracing the world with gentle love,
As daylight fades and darkness entwines.
A touch of orange, a fiery hue,
A kiss of warmth before the night,
A vibrant glow, a promise anew,
Filling the sky with a captivating light.
And there, amidst the colors so rare,
The gentle strokes of grey appear,
Soft wisps of clouds, floating with care,
Adding depth to the sky's frontier.
Oh, pastel sky, a breathtaking sight,
A symphony of colors, harmonious and true,
A reminder that beauty can take flight,
In every moment, in every hue.
So let us pause and admire this scene,
The sky's masterpiece, a gift from above,
A stunning display, forever serene,
A testament to nature's boundless love.

*2023*

# THE SKY LIGHT

In the sky, the Sun stands tall,
Casting its light upon us all.
A beacon of warmth, a guiding ray,
The Sun lite light that never fades away.
From dawn to dusk, it shines so bright,
Illuminating the world with its golden light.
It brings us hope, it brings us cheer,
Dispelling darkness, calming any fear.
The Sun lite light, a constant presence,
A reminder of life's endless essence.
It paints the sky with hues of gold,
A masterpiece that never grows old.
So let us bask in its radiant glow,
Embrace the warmth, let our spirits flow.
For the Sun lite light will always stay,
Guiding us through each and every day.

_Tony Mauk 2023_

# THE SUNSET

As the sun begins to descend,
The west coast comes alive,
A canvas of colors, a sight to behold,
Nature's magic, so vivid and bold.
The sky ablaze with hues so grand,
A masterpiece painted by nature's hand,
Shades of orange, pink, and gold,
A sunset story yet to be told.
The waves crash gently upon the shore,
Whispering secrets of the ocean's lore,
The salty breeze kisses my face,
In this moment, time and worries erase.
I stand in awe, humbled by the view,
Grateful for this moment, so pure and true,
Another day bids farewell, with grace,
As the sun sets, leaving a trace.
Awestruck by the beauty that unfolds,
Another magical sunset on the west coast,
I cherish these moments, forever I'll keep,
In my heart, a memory, so deep.

*2023*

# 911

In the depths of memory, they remain,
The echoes of a day filled with pain.
The morning of 9/11, forever etched in our hearts,
A tragedy that tore lives apart.
But amidst the sorrow, a glimmer of light,
As the morning Sun rises, shining so bright.
A canvas of orange, majestic and grand,
Painting the sky with a heavenly hand.
Though the scars may linger, the pain still near,
The beauty of the sunrise helps us persevere.
For in the face of darkness, hope finds its way,
Reminding us to cherish each new day.
So let us remember the morning so clear,
And honor the lives we hold dear.
For in the midst of tragedy, love will prevail,
And the morning Sun's glory will never fail.

---

*9-11 2023*

Public Domain.

# THE CANVAS SKY

In the early morn, as the sun does rise,
A canvas of orange fills the skies.
A sight so breathtaking, it takes my breath away,
Another beautiful morning, a brand-new day.
The hues of orange dance with golden light,
Painting the world with pure delight.
The sky ablaze with vibrant tones,
A symphony of colors, nature's own.
As the sun ascends, casting its gentle glow,
I feel a sense of peace, a tranquil flow.
The world awakens, bathed in this warm embrace,
A reminder of life's beauty, a moment to embrace.
So let us cherish this morning's orange sky,
A gift from nature, a sight that can't deny,
The magic and wonder that each day can bring,
In this world of beauty, let our hearts sing.

*September 2023*

# WILLIAMSBURG 1760

In times of challenge, do not despair,
For greatness emerges, a fervent affair.
Three great minds gather, at the table again,
Organizing a new culture, where ideas remain.
The sound of progress, a symphony of thought,
As routines of structure are diligently sought.
A society yet to unfold, in its grand design,
Virginia's Trinity of Immortals, so divine.
Washington, a leader with strength and might,
Jefferson, a visionary, shining bright,
And Henry, with words that ignite the flame,
Together they shape a nation's noble aim.
Their legacy echoes through the ages,
Inspiring generations, turning history's pages.
In their wisdom and courage, we find our way,
Forever grateful for their guiding ray.
So let us honor these great souls,
Whose visions and principles make us whole.
Virginia's Trinity, forever revered,
Their ideals and spirit, always endeared.

Courtesy of Colonial Williamsburg.

# A CHILD'S MIND

A child's busy mind unfolds and wants to reach out with love that never ceases.
What happens at 2:00 am even surprises me!
So where do all these words come from, they dance in the air?
Are they from aging minds or creative souls?
Or is it our spirits that connect us, the goal?
From deep within, they rise and take flight,
Born of experiences, emotions, and insight.
They flow like a river, swift and free,
Expressing thoughts and feelings, for all to see.
Sometimes they come from a place of pain,
Seeking solace, hoping to regain.
Other times, they burst forth with joy,
Celebrating life, like a child's toy.
They are the threads that weave our stories,
Painting pictures of our triumphs and glories.
They connect us, across time and space,
Creating bonds that no one can erase.
So let them dance, let them soar,
These words that we forever adore.
For they are the essence of our being,
A testament to the human heart's meaning.

_2023_

# A POEM OF DREAMS!

In the realm of dreams, where wonders unfold,
God's creation revealed, a story untold.
Lost family members, they reappear,
In nighttime conversations, their love so dear.
Their presence, so grand, fills the midnight air,
A reminder of love, beyond time and despair.
Miracles abound, in the stillness of night,
Colors so vivid, a celestial sight.
How many miracles, here and now,
In dreams, we find them, we humbly bow.
The colors of the night, so ever clear,
Gifts of beauty, banishing all fear.
So cherish the dreams, the whispers of grace,
Where loved ones reside, in that sacred space.
For in our slumber, God's love is revealed,
A tapestry of blessings, forever sealed.

_____

*2023*

# A FATHER AND HIS SON

My friend Bob and his only son John
In a father's eyes, a tale unfolds,
Of a precious child, with a future untold.
Though the odds may be stacked, against all belief,
Hope shines bright, bringing solace and relief.
Through tear-filled eyes, strength does arise,
A beacon of courage, that never dies.
With each passing moment, they hold on tight,
To the glimmer of hope, that guides them through the night.
In the face of despair, they find a way,
To embrace the unknown, and keep fears at bay.
For love knows no bounds, it perseveres,
In the face of adversity, it conquers all fears.
So let us stand beside them, in this trying hour,
Offering support, love, and a comforting shower.
For in the depths of a father's hopeful gaze,
We witness the power of love's eternal blaze.

# THE BEACON OF LOVE

In a world that can sometimes feel like a ghetto,
Where struggles and hardships may seem to grow,
There's still a glimmer of hope, shining bright,
A beacon of love, guiding us through the night.
In this house, sweet and nice,
We'll break the chains of sacrifice,
For those who have not, we'll lend a hand,
Sharing their heartache, together we'll stand.
For in unity, we find our strength,
Building bridges, breaking down the fence,
A better place, we'll create, hand in hand,
Where love and compassion will forever expand.
So let's hold onto hope, never let it go,
In this world that can sometimes feel like a ghetto,
With kindness and empathy, we'll rise above,
And transform this world into a place of love.

# GOODBYE JIMMY BUFFET

You brought us paradise
With hamburgers in hand, we felt so nice
Flip flops and bottle tops, oh so exotic
Transporting us to islands, so hypnotic
Your songs and images, a tropical escape
Taking us away from life's problems and shape
We danced and we sang, carefree and light
In your melodies, our worries took flight
Oh, the happy times we had, lost in your tunes
Drinking margaritas under the shining moon
You painted a picture of a life so serene
Where worries were forgotten, and troubles unseen
So farewell, Jimmy Buffet, thank you for the ride
For the moments of bliss, you've placed inside
Your music will forever bring us back
To those sunny shores, where our hearts unpack.

_____

*RIP Jimmy! 2023*

# FRIENDS FROM THE PAST

In the depths of memories, friends from the past,
A bond that time cannot ever outlast.
Roanoke Virginia, a place left behind,
Yet forever etched in the corners of my mind.
Age may keep ticking, but it never defines,
The friendships we cherish, like sparkling wine.
Mistakes may have been made, regrets may ensue,
But the care and love of true friends remain true.
Through ups and downs, they've stood by my side,
Through laughter and tears, they've been my guide.
In moments of darkness, they've brought me light,
A beacon of support, shining so bright.
So here's to those friends, so loyal and dear,
Whose presence in my life brings joy and cheer.
Though miles may separate us, our bond will stay,
Forever in my heart, come what may.

_August 2023_

# PUEBLO INDIANS

In the land of Pueblo, where traditions run deep,
A dance of corn, a celebration to keep.
With feathers and colors, the dancers unite,
To honor the harvest, under the sun's golden light.
Their feet stomp the earth, in rhythm and grace,
As the corn sways gently, in its sacred space.
The drums beat strong, echoing through the air,
As the community gathers, in love and care.
The dancers move with purpose, their steps so precise,
Telling stories of ancestors, with every rise.
The corn, a symbol of sustenance and life,
Nurtured by the earth, through struggle and strife.
With every twirl and spin, they honor the land,
Thanking the spirits, for their guiding hand.
The Pueblo corn dance, a beautiful sight,
A tribute to heritage, shining bright.
So let us join in, with hearts full of cheer,
Embracing the culture, that's held dear.
In the land of Pueblo, where traditions thrive,
We celebrate the corn dance, keeping it alive.

*2023 to the Pueblo children*

Courtesy of Indian Pueblo Cultural Center

# ACOMA INDIANS

In the land of Acoma, high in the sky,
A pueblo stands, where spirits fly.
Native roots run deep, through time untold,
A sacred place, with stories to unfold.
Do not let me be forgotten, I plea,
For my history is rich, as you can see.
Though bitter the mistreatment I've faced,
My nature is forgiveness, love embraced.
I am the Acoma, resilient and strong,
Through trials and tribulations, I belong.
With open arms, I welcome and share,
The beauty of my culture, beyond compare.
Let my spirit soar, like the eagle above,
In unity and harmony, bound by love.
For in the land of Acoma, I reside,
A native heritage, forever by my side.

---

*August 2023 to the beautiful souls that I embrace!*

# REFLECTIONS

As the moon cast its reflection on the ocean,
A dance of light and shadows begins in motion.
The waves glisten with a silver hue,
A magical scene, both tranquil and true.
The moonbeams caress the gentle tide,
Creating a path where dreams collide.
Whispers of secrets carried on the breeze,
A symphony of nature that puts the mind at ease.
In this moment, the world seems still,
As the moon and ocean embrace with skill.
A celestial love story, forever entwined,
A sight that leaves no heart behind.
So let us bask in this ethereal sight,
As the moon and ocean unite in the night.
May it remind us of life's beauty and grace,
And fill our hearts with awe and embrace.

*Aug 2023*

# FRIENDSHIPS

In the world of friendship, strong and true,
There stands a pillar, unwavering and true.
A column of support, in times of strife,
A beacon of hope, throughout this life.
Like a building, sturdy and grand,
It represents the strength we lend a hand.
For in our lives, we strive to be,
A constant support, for those in need.
Through thick and thin, we stand tall,
To lift others up, when they may fall.
With open arms, and hearts so kind,
We offer solace, to troubled minds.
So let us be pillars, firm and strong,
Building bridges, where they belong.
For in supporting others, we find our worth,
A legacy of love, that will traverse the earth.

---

*August 2023*

# THE LIGHT OF THE DAY

In the light of day, the world awakes,
With golden rays, the sun partakes.
Nature dances, in vibrant hues,
As morning's light, brings life anew.
The birds take flight, their songs so sweet,
A symphony of melodies, a joyous treat.
The flowers bloom, in colors bright,
A tapestry of beauty, a pure delight.
The gentle breeze, whispers in the air,
Caressing cheeks, with a tender care.
The sky above, so vast and blue,
A canvas of dreams, for me and you.
In the light of day, let worries fade,
Embrace the warmth, let happiness cascade.
For each new dawn, brings endless possibility,
In the light of day, let your spirit roam free.

_____

*Aug 2023*

# BROKEN HEARTS

My heart was broken in 1990 and I fled this town,
But I soon realized that I was wrong,
For the place I call home is a healing ground,
Where I can lay my burdens down.
The people here are so warm and kind,
Their love and support I can't deny,
It's here I can look up to the sky,
And begin to heal and learn to fly.
The beauty of nature, the rolling hills,
The sunlit meadows and the stillness of night,
Are the perfect place to find peace of mind,
And start to mend my broken heart, so I can take flight.

---

*2023*

# LOST LOVE

My love for you is crystal clear
Drifting further away, day after day
The memories of you, they never fade
I close my eyes and I can see
Your smile shining bright, so vividly
The nights are long, the days are slow
But I know one day, you'll come back home
And until then, I'll keep holding on
To the love we shared, so strong
Oh, can't you see it, my dear?
My love for you is crystal clear
Wherever you go, whatever you do
I'll be right here, thinking of you
Whatever it takes, however my heart breaks
I'll be forever near, thinking of you
For in the end, our love will survive
And together, we'll thrive.
So drifting further away, my love, and don't look back
I'll be here, thinking of you, my heart intact
For in the end, our love will find a way
And we'll be together, forever and a day.

---

*July 1981*

# HOPELESS LOVE

A love so sweet, so pure and true
From the hills of Palos Verdes
A love that blossomed and grew
A love that was meant to be
In the warmth of the summer sun
We shared a love that was so much fun
An everlasting bond that would never be undone
Our love was strong, our love was real
We laughed and we danced, we sang and we played
We shared our dreams and our hopes that day
And when the night came, we'd sit and we'd sway
Our love was strong, our love was real
Though time has passed and things have changed
The memory of that love still remains
It's a reminder of a love that will never fade
Our love was strong, our love was real.

*Tony Mauk 2023*

# WILD FLOWERS

The Wild Flowers
The wild flowers of Palos Verdes
Are a sight for sore eyes
A splash of color in the sky
As the sun begins to rise
The yellow, orange, and blues
Bring a smile to my face
The beauty of nature here
Is a special place

_____

*2003*

# PALOS VERDES

Palos Verdes, oh how you inspire
With your beauty that never tires
From the sunsets that light up the sky
To the stars that twinkle up high
Your cliffs and beaches are so grand
With views that take our breath away
The ocean waves that crash on the sand
Make us want to stay and play
At night, your lights shimmer and glow
A sight to see, a beautiful show
The moon and stars, they dance and shine
A perfect end to a day so divine
Palos Verdes, you are a sight to behold
A place of wonder, a story untold
Forever in our hearts, you'll stay
A place we'll cherish, come what may.

*April 1999*

# THE CLIFFS OF PALOS VERDES

A sight so grand and so grandiose,
Our Creator's wondrous hand,
Gave us this beauty to behold.
The waves crashing on the shore,
The sand, the rocks, and the trees,
This place of beauty galore,
A sight that will never cease.
The sunsets, the stars, the sky,
Our Creator's work on display,
A sight that will never die,
A beauty seen each and every day.

*2023*

# FOGGY NIGHT AT SEA

The foggy night out on the sea,
The thunder and the lightning,
The foghorns in the distance,
A stormy sight to see.
The waves crashing against the shore,
The raindrops pitter-patter,
The misty air, the salty spray,
A wild and wondrous matter.
The chill in the air, the darkness so deep,
The thunder and lightning, so loud and so steep,
The foghorns in the distance,
A thunderous symphony,
A beautiful sight to behold out on the sea.

_____

*1990*

# THE GLASS CHURCH

The glass church stands so tall,
Its beauty captivates the soul.
The glass shimmers and glows,
A peaceful sight to behold.
The light that it casts is divine,
It's beauty so hard to define.
The glass church calls us to come,
A place of beauty, peace and love.

*2023*

# THE FOG

The night is still, the air is moist
The sound of foghorns, a haunting voice
The whipper will, it echoes far
A symphony of sounds, a nocturnal memoir.

*April 2023*

# THE WAVES

The melody of the waves,
A gentle sound that soothes,
The crashing of the shore,
A calming rhythm that moves.
The ocean's song so sweet,
A lullaby of peace,
The sound of the tide,
A gentle balm to ease.

*2003*

# ROESSLER POINT

The sun is setting,
the sky is turning pink,
The waves are crashing,
On the shore of Roessler Point.
The breeze is blowing,
The birds are singing,
The sand is glistening,
In the fading light.
The world is so peaceful,
The air so still,
The beauty around me,
Makes my heart thrill.
The ocean is vast,
The horizon wide,
The beauty of nature,
Fills me with pride.
The sun has now set,
The sky is dark blue,
But the memories of Roessler Point,
Will forever stay with me.

*2003*

# THE MONARCH BUTTERFLY

Fluttering wings of gold and black,
Monarch butterflies, a natural knack,
In the breeze they dance and play,
A sight to see, a perfect display.
From flower to flower they roam,
Drinking nectar, a sweet home,
A symbol of beauty and grace,
Monarch butterflies, a true embrace.
Their journey long, their path unknown,
A migration like no other shown,
A wonder of nature, a true delight,
Monarch butterflies, a majestic sight.

*2016*

# NEIGHBORHOOD CHURCH

Neighborhood church, a place to find solace and release.
The trees whispered their secrets, the peacocks sang their songs,
A place of refuge, where I could belong.
The sun shone bright, the sky so clear,
A place to find hope, and to shed a tear.
The wind blew softly, the clouds moved on by,
A place to heal, and to find my sigh.

*2023*

# THE GATE

In the realm of endless possibilities, behold,
Stands the door of time, a story yet untold.
With hinges creaking, it beckons us near,
Inviting us to conquer our doubts and fear.

Step through its threshold, brave and bold,
To journey through the ages, as legends foretold.
Behind lies the past, a tapestry of memories,
Whispering secrets and forgotten histories.

Or venture forth into the future unknown,
Where dreams and aspirations have yet to be sown.
Embrace the winds of change, let them guide,
As you shape the destiny that waits inside.

For within this door, time's eternal embrace,
Lies the power to transform, to find your place.
Embrace the lessons of the past, let them guide,
As you craft a future where your dreams reside.

So walk through the door, with heart and mind,
Embrace the adventure that you will find.
Through the door of time, your path will unfold,
Embracing the change, as stories are told.

---

*2023 July 26*

# NINETEEN PUEBLOS

In the heart of New Mexico's land,
Lies a tapestry so grand,
Nineteen Pueblos strong and true,
Preserving traditions, old and new.

With humble hearts and spirits bright,
They welcome all, day and night,
Their love for life, so pure and clear,
Shines through their laughter, so sincere.

Their dances tell stories of ancient days,
Their songs echo through the sunlit haze,
Their sorrows run deep, yet they endure,
With resilience and strength, forever secure.

Oh, Pueblos of New Mexico, I am in awe,
Of your wisdom, your grace, and the love you draw,
Thank you for sharing your ways with me,
A glimpse into a world so rich and free.

May your traditions forever thrive,
As you keep your culture alive,
In every step, in every beat,
Your spirit shines, ever so sweet.

_____

*July 2023*

# RINCON LN PALOS VERDES ESTATES, CA

The Queens Necklace, a sight so grand
A shimmering string of lights along the sand
A reminder of a regal past
A reminder of the beauty that shall last
The Queens Necklace, a sight so bright
A magical sight that illuminates the night
A reminder of a distant shore
A reminder of the love that will endure!

*1977 -Written in Memory for my dear friend Silvia Reynes*

# THE STARS TWINKLE IN THE NIGHT

We laugh and giggle 'till daylight
Our first sleepover, so much fun
We'll never forget when it's done
We talk and share secrets, all night long
We stay up 'till the morning comes along
It's a night of friendship, laughter and glee
Our first sleepover, just you and me

*2022*

# OCEAN WAVES

The ocean waves crash and roar
The blue sky and sun set the shore
The white sand and clear blue sea
Palos Verdes views are a sight to see

*2023*

# FOG

Fog so thick, obscuring the view
May Gray and June Gloom, what can we do?
A chill creeps in, a blanket of gray
The sun hides away, a misty display

*1989*

# PV IN THE 70'S

Fast cars and bright lights,
A place to find freedom,
Palos Verdes in the 70's,
A fast lane of life in front of you.

Racing through the night,
The sound of engines at full throttle,
The stars above,
A never-ending journey to explore.

The smell of the sea,
The feeling of the wind in your hair,
The thrill of the ride,
Nothing can compare.

Fast cars and bright lights,
A place to find freedom,
Palos Verdes in the 70's,
A fast lane of life in front of you.

*1977*

# BIRDS

Beautiful birds with colors so bright
The rainbow of feathers so light
From the blue jays to the cardinals
To the finches and the sparrows
Bringing joy to the morning skies
As they soar and they fly
Beautiful birds with colors so bright
A sight that never fails to delight

*2008*

# A PEACOCK'S BEAUTY

A peacock's beauty, so grand and free,
Strolling through Palos Verdes Estates,
A regal sight for all to see,
This is a beauty that never abates.
A rainbow of colors, so bright and bold,
A sight that can never be sold,
A shimmering display of grace untold,
A peacock's beauty, a sight to behold.

*1982*

# LA LOVE

Through the highs and lows, we'll survive
Together we'll conquer mountains high
Our love will never die

I was standing by myself
Los Angeles around me felt so far from home
But then you came and gave me hope
A light in the darkness, a way to cope

And now we're standing side by side
Our love is strong, we cannot hide
The world is ours, we'll take the ride
Our love will keep us alive.

*1977*

# MARCH WINDS

March winds blow high and wild,
Kites fly in the sky so mild.
Waves crash against the shore,
Children laugh and play evermore.

*2023*

# THE WHALES

The whales come from the deep,
To grace the shores of Palos Verdes.
Migration so grand and so wide,
Their journey is long, but they abide.

Their beauty and grace, a sight to behold,
A sight to cherish and never grow old.
From the depths of the sea, they come to show,
The majesty of nature, a sight to behold.

*2003*

# PEOPLE

People from near and far,
Come together to Palos Verdes shores,
A place of beauty and peace,
Where we can all find our home.

From different lands, different cultures,
We share our stories and dreams,
In the spirit of unity,
We create a place of harmony.

No matter where we come from,
We are one in this special place,
We are the people of Palos Verdes,
A special place of grace.

---

*2003*

# SEAGULL IN THE SKY

The seagull soars high in the sky,
The sun blazing bright in the sky,
The seagull glides in the air,
The sun warming the air.

The seagull and sun in harmony,
The seagull and sun in unity,
The seagull and sun in perfect harmony,
A beautiful sight for all to see.

*2014*

# FOG ON THE SHORE

Fog shrouds the shore,
The waves crash and roar,
Palos Verdes Estates' beauty shines evermore.
The morning mist rolls in,
A view of the sea,
The tranquil beauty of nature to see.

*2023*

# NEPTUNE'S FOUNTAIN

In the heart of Malaga Cove Plaza,
A fountain stands tall and proud,
It's been here since 1930,
And it's Neptune's Fountain, so loud.

The King of the Sea stands tall and proud,
His trident in hand, a symbol of power,
His gaze is stern and his face is proud,
He stands tall in the evening hour.

The water sprays from Neptune's trident,
It glistens in the sun,
It's a sight of beauty and grandeur,
For everyone to come.
The fountain stands tall and proud,
It's been here since 1930,
It's a reminder of Neptune's power,
And a reminder of the sea's might and strength.

_____

*1998*

# MUSIC IN THE WATER

The melody of the waves,
A gentle sound that soothes,
The crashing of the shore,
A calming rhythm that moves.

The ocean's song so sweet,
A lullaby of peace,
The sound of the tide,
A gentle balm to ease.

*2003*

# OUR LOCAL NEIGHBORS-SEA TURTLES!

Oh sea turtles, so majestic and free
Your graceful swimming, so effortless to see
Your shells so beautiful, your eyes so wise
You bring us joy, and teach us to be wise

Your population is threatened, so sad to see
We must help you, friends of the sea
So let us protect you, with all our might
And keep your species swimming in the night

*2021*

# ENDLESS SKIES

In the vast canvas of endless skies,
Where nature's artistry truly lies,
A symphony of colors starts to unfold,
Painting stories, both new and old.

Patel blues, like whispers of dreams,
Embrace the heavens in gentle streams,
While squirls of orange, a fiery dance,
Illuminate the sky in a vibrant trance.

In those precious moments, morning or late,
When sunrays pierce through heaven's gate,
A kaleidoscope of hues, a glorious array,
Reveals the mood of nature's display.

For on stormy days, when dark clouds brew,
The sky weeps tears of a somber hue,
Raindrops fall, like nature's gentle plea,
Washing the world, setting spirits free.

And when the wind howls with wild delight,
Clouds race across the canvas, taking flight,
Their shapes and forms, ever-changing, grand,
Creating masterpieces across the land.

The best paintings, indeed, are filled with clouds,
Whispering secrets, their mysteries allowed,
They add depth and character to the scene,
Transforming the ordinary into the serene.

So let us marvel at the sky's painted grace,
The ever-shifting palette nature embraces,
For in those fleeting moments of divine art,
We find solace and wonder in our heart.

# OCTOBER SKIES

The horizon becomes an artist's dream,
A masterpiece that makes hearts gleam,
Silhouettes of trees stand tall,
Admiring nature's grand curtain call.

As the sun dips below the edge,
The sky becomes a starlit pledge,
A symphony of colors, a fleeting sight,
Leaving memories that shine so bright.

Oh, majestic sunsets, you captivate,
A moment of pure awe, we celebrate,
With each stroke of divine art,
You ignite the depths of every heart.

So let us pause and take it in,
Let the beauty of the sunset begin,
For in these fleeting moments, we find,
An eternal connection with humankind.

In the splendor of the evening's glow,
Nature's masterpiece, it does bestow,
The gift of serenity, joy, and peace,
In the majestic sunsets, our souls find release.

# AUTHOR BIO

**Anthony "Tony" Mauk** is an accomplished engineer, business leader, and community advocate who also pursues his passion for the written word. Although known for his technological innovations and managerial expertise, Tony finds inspiration and solace in poetry, regularly penning verses that provide a window into his innermost thoughts.

As president of Siliconia Technologies, Tony draws on decades of experience spearheading advancements in telecommunications. However, in his leisure time, he taps into his creative side, channeling his emotions into heartfelt poems. Writing provides Tony with a creative outlet to process life's complexities.

The grandfather of 13 cherishes opportunities to impart wisdom to future generations. Tony often weaves tales of his rich experiences into lyrical compositions. Through vivid language and evocative imagery, his poems elucidate poignant lessons and hard-won knowledge.

Tony's affinity for language also shines through in his community leadership. As a champion for empowering indigenous populations, he recognizes the power of narrative and self-expression. His support for Smart Tribe Technologies, which assists Native American communities through technology and entrepreneurship, demonstrates his appreciation for uplifting voices.

With an insatiable intellectual curiosity and passion for the written word, Tony Mauk continues to find inspiration all around him. Whether reflecting on relationships, nature's beauty, or his remarkable journey, Tony's poignant verses give readers a window into the insight, compassion, and visionary perspective that define this multidimensional leader.

www.ingramcontent.com/pod-product-compliance
Lightning Source LLC
Chambersburg PA
CBHW041514120626
46551CB00018B/2419